PHONICS Reading Program

by Quinlan B. Lee

SCHOLASTIC INC.
New York Toronto London Auckland Sydney
Mexico City New Delhi Hong Kong Buenos Aires

Designed by Jenn Martino

Go, Diego, Go!™: Baby Jaguar Can! (0-439-91305-5) © 2007 Viacom International Inc.
Go, Diego, Go! ™: Out of the Nest (0-439-91306-3) © 2007 Viacom International Inc.
Go, Diego, Go!™: Quick! Help the Fish! (0-439-91307-1) © 2007 Viacom International Inc.
Go, Diego, Go!™: Hop Like a Tree Frog (0-439-91308-X) © 2007 Viacom International Inc.
Go, Diego, Go!™: Stuck in the Mud (0-439-91309-8) © 2007 Viacom International Inc.
Go, Diego, Go!™: Time to Sleep (0-439-91310-1) © 2007 Viacom International Inc.
Go, Diego, Go!™: The Rain Forest Race (0-439-91311-X) © 2007 Viacom International Inc.
Go, Diego, Go!™: Ice Is Nice (0-439-91312-8) © 2007 Viacom International Inc.
Go, Diego, Go!™: Let's Go See Holes! (0-439-91313-6) © 2007 Viacom International Inc.
Go, Diego, Go!™: The Great Dinosaur Rescue (0-439-91314-4) © 2007 Viacom International Inc.
Go, Diego, Go!™: Shadow Show (0-439-91315-2) © 2007 Viacom International Inc.
Go, Diego, Go!™: Chinta the Chinchilla (0-439-91316-0) © 2007 Viacom International Inc.

ISBN-13: 978-0545-01372-7
ISBN: 0-545-01372-0

12 11 10 9 8 7 6 5 4 3 2 1   7 8 9 10 11/0

Printed in Singapore
This compilation edition first printing, June 2007

• Table of Contents •

In this story, you can learn all about the short "a" sound. Here are some words to sound out.

can   clap   past   grab   fast   that

These are words that you will see in this story and many other stories. You will want to learn them as well.

him   he   jump   to   you

These are some more challenging words that you will see in this story.

jaguar   climb   mountain
blowing   high   hooray

PHONICS Reading Program

Baby Jaguar Can!

by Quinlan B. Lee

Can Baby **Jaguar** climb
to the top of the mountain?
Let's climb with him
and Mommy **Jaguar**!
Grab the zip cord
and **clap** your hands.
Clap, clap, clap!

The wind is blowing **fast**.
Crash!
Oh, no! A tree fell on
the **path**.
How **can** we get **past** it?

Welcome to the **Go, Diego, Go!** Phonics Reading Program!

Learning to read is so important for your child's success in school and in life. Now **Diego** is here to help your child learn important phonics skills.

Phonics is the fundamental skill of knowing that the letters we read represent the sounds we hear and say. **Diego** helps your child LEARN to read and LOVE to read!

Here's how these readers work:

- At first you may want to read the story to your child.

- Then read together by taking turns line by line or page by page.

- Encourage your child to read the story independently.

- Look for all the words that have the sound being featured in the reader. Read them over and over again.

Scholastic has been encouraging young readers for more than 80 years. Thank you for letting us help you support your beginning reader.

Happy reading,

Francie Alexander
Chief Academic Officer, Scholastic Inc.

We **can** swing on this vine.
We **can** swing **past** the tree.
But how **can** the **jaguars**
get **past** the tree?

Jaguars are **cats that can** jump high.
They **can** jump **past** the tree.
Can you jump like a **jaguar**?
Stand up and jump!

Can you see Baby **Jaguar**?
Jaguars can blend in well.
Look for **tan** and **brown**.
Can you find him?
No, **that** is a bird.

There he is!

Jaguars can run **fast**.

Can you run **fast**, too?

Stand up and run!

Run **fast, fast, fast**!

Baby **Jaguar**, jump to
the top!
You **can** do it!
Let's **clap** and say,
"You **can** do it!"
Clap, clap, clap!

Baby **Jaguar can** get to the top! Hooray!

In this story, you can learn all about the short "e" sound. Here are some words to sound out.

help   egg   check   nest   fell   yes

These are words that you will see in this story and many other stories. You will want to learn them as well.

four   two   they   no   from

These are some more challenging words that you will see in this story.

**toucans   tropic   crocodile
another   build   leave**

PHONICS Reading Program

Out of the Nest

by Quinlan B. Lee

The toucans need **help**!
They had four **eggs**
in their **nest**.
One, two, three.
Oh, no! An **egg fell** from
the **nest**!

Check next to those rocks.

Is there an **egg**? **Yes!**

Is it a toucan **egg**?

Let's check.

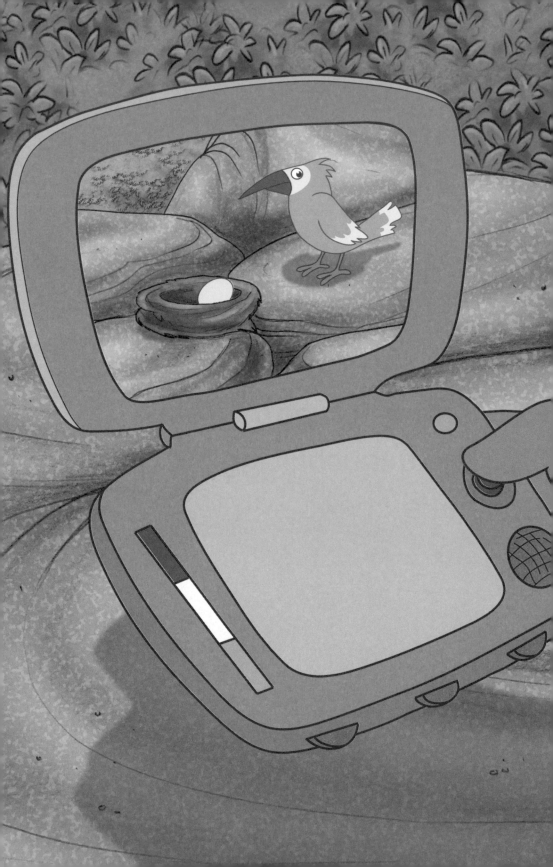

Toucans make **nests** in trees, not **next** to rocks. A **red**-billed tropic bird makes **nests next** to rocks. It is her **egg**.

Check next to the lake.

Is there an **egg**? **Yes!**

Is it a toucan **egg**?

Let's check!

Crocodiles make **nests** **next** to lakes.
This **egg** is a crocodile **egg**.
It is **best** to leave it alone.

There is another **egg**.
It is **next** to that tree.
Is it a toucan **egg**?
Let's check!

Yes! Toucans build **nests**
in trees.
Toco, here is your **egg**.
Now you can put it back
in your **nest**.

We did it! Now the **eggs** are in the **nest**.

In this story, you can learn all about the short "i" sound. Here are some words to sound out.

ship   **skin**   **snip**   **fish**   **fin**   **gills**

These are words that you will see in this story and many other stories. You will want to learn them as well.

we   **on**   **about**   **find**   **hard**

These are some more challenging words that you will see in this story.

learn   **trouble**   **coral**
breathe   **water**   **stretch**

PHONICS Reading Program

Quick! Help the Fish!

by Quinlan B. Lee

We are on a **ship**
to learn about **fish**.
A **fish is in** trouble.
Quick, Click! Help us
find **it**.

It is a frog **fish**.

Frog **fish** are hard to see.

Their **skin** blends **in with** the coral.

Look! His **fin is** stuck **in** a net.

We need to **snip** the net.

How **will** we breathe
in the water?
Fish use their **gills**.
We need something
like **fish gills** so we can
swim in the water.

Rescue Pack can help!
He can turn **into** an air tank.
Now we can breathe like
we have **fish gills**.
Quick! We need to help
the **fish**.

Fish swim with their fins.
Let's swim to the fish.
Quick! Stretch out your
hands and swim, swim,
swim!

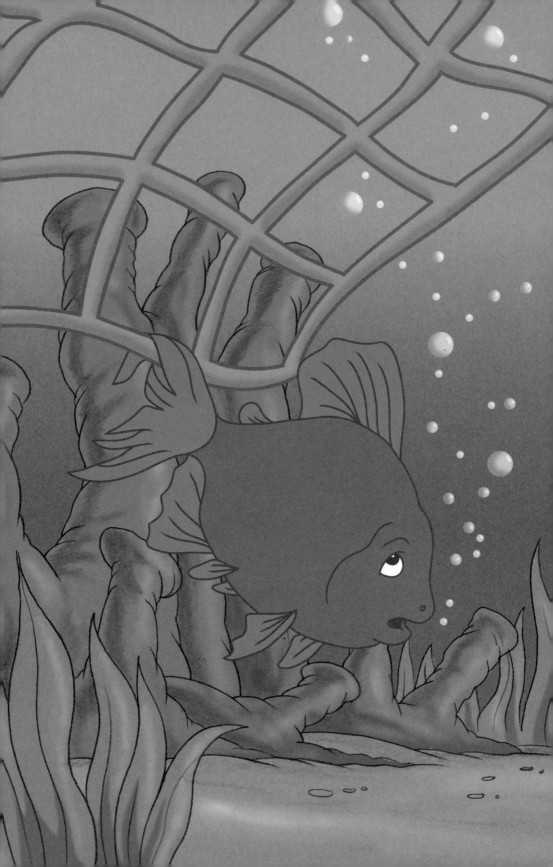

Do you see the frog **fish**?
His skin blends **in**.
His fin is stuck **in** the net.
He cannot **snip** the net to
get free.

How can we **snip** the net?
Clippers!
Let's **snip with** the
clippers.
Snip, snip, snip!

We **did it**! Look at the **fish swim**!

In this story, you can learn all about the short "o" sound. Here are some words to sound out.

frog   stop   hop   log   drop   top

These are words that you will see in this story and many other stories. You will want to learn them as well.

our   are   going   must   have

These are some more challenging words that you will see in this story.

river	**coconut**	**pyramid**
gloves	**climb**	**jaguar**

PHONICS Reading Program

Hop Like a Tree Frog!

by Quinlan B. Lee

The red-eyed tree **frogs** need our help!
The **frogs** are **on** a **log** going down the river.
The **log** will **not stop**.

The wind is making the
ChaCha Coconut Trees
drop their coconuts.
Hop like a tree **frog**
so they will **not drop on** us!
Hop, hop, hop!

Do you **spot** the tree **frogs**?
There they are!
We must **stop** the **log**!
It is going into the pyramid.

Do you **spot** the door?
Look! It is at the **top**.
How can we get to the **top**?
I have gloves that stick
like tree **frog** toes.

We can climb to the **top**
like a tree **frog**.
Hop on, Baby Jaguar.
Let's climb to the
top, top, top!

Now do you **spot** the tree **frogs**?
Quick! We must **stop** the **log**.
We do **not** have a **lot** of time!

Tree **frogs, hop** off your **log**
to the **top** of this **rock**.
Hop, hop, hop!
Hop to this **rock**!

We **got** the tree **frogs**!

In this story, you can learn all about the short "u" sound. Here are some words to sound out.

yummy   **stuck**   **up**   **but**   **mud**   **hum**

These are words that you will see in this story and many other stories. You will want to learn them as well.

in   **it**   **or**   **is**   **have**

These are some more challenging words that you will see in this story.

llama   **basket**   **mountain**
fair   **where**   **stretch**

PHONICS Reading Program

Stuck in the Mud

by Quinlan B. Lee

Linda the Llama has
a basket of **yummy** food.
She is taking it
up the mountain and
to the fair.
But she is **stuck** in
the **mud**!

Where is Linda?
Llamas like to **hum**.
Let's **hum** like a llama
so Linda can find **us**.
Hum, hum, hum!

I hear Linda **hum**.

Which path leads to Linda?

Yes! Let's go **up** that path.

Hum so Linda can hear **us**.

Hum, hum, hum!

We found her!
Yuck! This **muck** is sticky.
Let's help Linda
get **unstuck** from the **mud**.

We did it!

But now the rope is **stuck**!

Is it **stuck** in the **mud** or

up in the tree?

How can we reach **up**
in the tree?
Llamas have long necks.
Stretch like a llama.
Up, up, up!

We did it!
We got Linda **unstuck**
from the **mud**
and made it **up** to the fair
with the **yummy** food.

Yum! This food is great!

In this story, you can learn all about the long "e" sound. Here are some words to sound out.

see   leaf   green   need   beak   sleep

These are words that you will see in this story and many other stories. You will want to learn them as well.

the   do   six   that   who

These are some more challenging words that you will see in this story.

**animals   flashlight   toucan
something   upside down   sloth**

PHONICS Reading Program

Time to Sleep

by Quinlan B. Lee

The sun is not up yet.
Let's **see** which animals
are still **sleeping**.

We **need** my flashlight to
see in that **tree**.
What do you **see** under
that **leaf**?
Do you **see** a **beak**?

Who do you **see**?

It is a toucan.

Is **he sleeping**?

Yes! Toucans **sleep** at night.

Do you **see** something **green** under that **leaf**? There are six **feet**. Whose **feet** are they?

I **see three tree** frogs.
They have six **feet**
and six red eyes.
They are not **sleeping**.
Tree frogs **sleep** in the day.

Did you **see**
something **peek** at us?
I **see** upside-down legs.
Who hangs upside down
in **trees**?

It is Sammy the Sloth.
He **sleeps** in the day
like the **tree** frogs.
Now I **see** the sun!
Do you know what that
means?

Good morning, toucans!
Sleep tight, Sammy and
tree frogs.

In this story, you can learn all about the long "a" sound. Here are some words to sound out.

race   shake   make   gate   pace   place

These are words that you will see in this story and many other stories. You will want to learn them as well.

goes   under   down   slow   fast

These are some more challenging words that you will see in this story.

armadillo	**cannot**	**muddy**
diggers	**might**	**finish**

Book 7
long a

PHONICS Reading Program

The Rain Forest Race

by Quinlan B. Lee

We are on Armadillo's
race team.
Let's get to the start **gate**.
Ready, set, **race**!

The **race** goes under the nut trees.

When the ground **quakes**, it **makes** the trees **shake**.

When the trees **shake**, the nuts fall.

When the trees **shake**, the nuts **make** the other teams slow down.
They cannot keep up their fast **pace**.
What can we do?

Yeah! Armadillo has
a hard shell.
Will you **make** a shell, too?
Lift up your arms and
make a shell!
We **made** it!

It is very muddy in
this **place**.
How can we **make** it
through the mud?
Armadillos are great
diggers!
She can **make** a path.

The other teams are fast!
They might **make** it
to the finish **gate** first.
How can we win the **race**?
What **shape** can Armadillo
make?

She can **make** a ball **shape** and roll to the finish **gate**. Curl up and **make** a ball. Roll, roll, roll!

We **made** it! We won
the **race!**

In this story, you can learn all about the long "i" sound. Here are some words to sound out.

ice **like** **slide** **dive** **ride** **bike**

These are words that you will see in this story and many other stories. You will want to learn them as well.

all **who** **do** **down** **on**

These are some more challenging words that you will see in this story.

Antarctica **penguin** **whale**
family **tummy** **helped**

PHONICS Reading Program

Ice Is Nice

by Quinlan B. Lee

Look at all the snow
and **ice**.
I am in Antarctica.
I am here to see penguins.

Penguins **like** snow and **ice**.
They **like** to **slide** on the **ice**.
They **like** to **dive** and swim.

Oh, no!
Baby Penguin did not
dive in.
He is too little to swim.
He is stuck out on the **ice**.
Who can help us?

The blue whale can help.
Blue whales **like** to swim.
I can **slide** on and **ride** to
Baby Penguin.

Now we must get
to Baby Penguin's family.
How can we cross the **ice**?

Baby Penguin can **slide** down the **ice** on his tummy. What do I need to **slide** down the **ice**? A **bike**? A **glider**?

I need a sled to **slide** down the **ice**. **Slide, slide, slide**!

We crossed the **ice** and helped Baby Penguin!

In this story, you can learn all about the long "o" sound. Here are some words to sound out.

hole   poke   home   scope   nose   close

These are words that you will see in this story and many other stories. You will want to learn them as well.

it   is   out   see   so

These are some more challenging words that you will see in this story.

**something   until   river
turtle   asleep   spider**

Book 9
long o

PHONICS Reading Program

Let's Go See Holes!

by Quinlan B. Lee

Let's **go** see **holes**!
Hold on and let's **go**!
Do you see any **holes**?
Use your **scope**.

Look, a **hole**!
Did you see something
poke out of the **hole**?
It is a big **nose**.

It is a paca!
He has a big **nose**.
He is asleep.
He does not **go** out
until the sun sets.

Use your **scope**
and look **close** to the river.
It is a **hole**.
Is this **hole** a **home**?
Let's **go** see!

Why is this **hole so close** to the river?
Let's read the **note**.
It is a river turtle nest.

Let's find one more **hole**.
Did you see something
poke out?
What do you think it is?
Is it a **mole**?

No! It is a spider.
This **hole** is his **home**.
He was asleep.
When the sun went down,
he **woke** up.

It is great to discover **holes**! Now it is time to **go home**.

In this story, you can learn all about the long "u" sound. Here are some words to sound out.

huge   clue   use   dune

These are words that you will see in this story and many other stories. You will want to learn them as well.

the   help   your   their   tail

These are some more challenging words that you will see in this story.

dinosaur   family   climb
watch   rescue   good-bye

GO DIEGO GO!

PHONICS Reading Program

The Great Dinosaur Rescue

by Quinlan B. Lee

The dinosaur is **huge**.

She could **use** our help.

She wants to find her family.

Where did her family go?
Do you see a **clue**?
There are prints in
the **dune**.

Those prints were
a good **clue**.
Now **use** the scope to
find her family.
We have to climb over
these **dunes** and go up
that **huge** slope.

Let's go over the **dunes**
and up the slope.
Watch out!
It is a rock slide.
What can we **use** that is soft
to land on?
Rescue Pack can help us!

Thanks, **Rescue** Pack!
Now let's **use** the dinosaur's
huge tail to climb back up to
her family.

Use your hands and
let's go!
Let's go up the **huge** tail.
We did it!

It is the dinosaur's family.
They are so big.
Look at their **huge** smiles
for their baby.

Good-bye, dinosaur.
We love to **rescue**!

In this story, you can learn all about the "sh" sound. Here are some words to sound out.

shadow   show   shiny   shapes   sheds   shell

These are words that you will see in this story and many other stories. You will want to learn them as well.

its   this   have   what   great

These are some more challenging words that you will see in this story.

animal	**better**	**armadillo**
slowly	**upside**	**sloth**

PHONICS Reading Program

Shadow Show

by Quinlan B. Lee

Let's play **shadow shapes**.
I'll **show** you how.
This animal **sheds** its skin.
What is it?

It is a snake.

It **sheds** its skin when
it grows.

Then it grows **shiny**
new skin.

What animal **shape** is this?
It has a hard **shell**.
It can dig better than a
shovel.

It is an armadillo.
Its **shell** protects its
soft body.
It digs with its **sharp** claws.

Whose **shadow** is this?
This animal moves slowly.
It likes to hang upside down.

It is a sloth.

Sloths are **shy**.

They have **sharp** claws.

What animal **shape** is this?
You ride in a **ship** to see
this animal.
It is a **fish** with **sharp** teeth.

It is a **shark**.

Great work!

In this story, you can learn all about the "ch" sound. Here are some words to sound out.

Chinta change reach choose chomp chinchilla

These are words that you will see in this story and many other stories. You will want to learn them as well.

our   over   into   now   have

These are some more challenging words that you will see in this story.

waterfall	**hungry**	**mountain**
rocky	**happy**	**glider**

GO DIEGO GO!

NICK JR.

PHONICS Reading Program

Chinta the Chinchilla

by Quinlan B. Lee

Chinta the **Chinchilla** needs our help.
She is on a **branch** over a waterfall.
We need to **catch** her!

Rescue Pack can **change**
to help us.
Will he **change** into a bike
or a hang glider?
You **choose**!

Now **reach** out and **catch**
Chinta the **Chinchilla**.
Reach, reach, reach!
We got her!

Chinta the **Chinchilla** is hungry.
Chinchillas eat plants.
Watch her **chomp**!

Let's take **Chinta** the **Chinchilla** home. **Chinchillas** live in the mountains. **Check** the scope for **Chinchilla** Mountain.

It is **chilly**.
Chinchillas have fur
to keep them warm.
I can keep warm
if I **change** my clothes.

Chinchilla Mountain is very rocky.
Chinchillas hop up the mountain.
Hop, hop, hop!

Chinta the **Chinchilla** is happy to be back on **Chinchilla** Mountain. Great work!